GW00650115

Exploring Fire and Clay

Arne Bjørn

Exploring
Fire and Clay

Man, Fire, and Clay Through the Ages

VNR Van Nostrand Reinhold Company
New York Cincinnati Toronto London Melbourne

Printed and bound in Great Britain by Jarrold & Sons Ltd,
Norwich

Published by Van Nostrand Reinhold Company
A Division of Litton Educational Publishing, Inc.
450 West 33rd Street, New York, New York, 10001
Published simultaneously in Canada by
D. Van Nostrand Company (Canada), Ltd

1 3 5 7 11 13 16 14 12 10 8 6 4 2

Contents

Photography

Palle F. Andersen: front cover, pages 12a, 17, 18, 24, 25, 33b, 39, 41, 43, 46, 47, 51, 52, 62, 72, 73
Arne Bjørn: pages 11, 13, 14a, 21, 22a, 34, 36, 49, 53, 56a–b, 58, 60, 63, 65, 68, 74, 77, 79
Dorrit Bjørn: page 27
The Open Air Museum, Lyngby, Denmark: pages 29, 32
Bent Josefsen: pages 22b, 40a–b, 64b, 81
Gunvor Jørsholm: pages 10, 33a
The Danish National Museum, Copenhagen, Denmark: pages 40, 54
Søren Mørch: pages 19, 45
Hakon Nielsen: page 28
Museum of Nimes, France: page 12b
The Museum of Schleswig-Holstein, Gottorp, West Germany: page 14b
Søren Sternø: page 16
The series on page 48 is from *Making Ceramics* (Van Nostrand Reinhold Company, New York).
(*a* refers to photographs in the text column, *b* refers to photographs in the margin.) Drawings and vignettes are by Arne Bjørn and Anne Josefsen.

Foreword

This book is an invitation for both adults and children to devote part of their spare time to experiencing the working methods of our forebears and to consider how much of our present high standard of living rests on the development of discoveries made by our remote ancestors.

It invites adults, parents, and teachers to act as constructive guides and counsellors for children and adolescents when their inherent urge toward experimentation leads them into one of the more dangerous areas of exploration such as fire. It invites the children to entice their parents to take part in their play with the ever-fascinating irresistible fire.

Adults will find that joining young people in their experiments with bonfires, primitive cooking, or making pottery will be a most interesting and rewarding activity, and a source of great pleasure for the entire group.

The experiments described here are based on the results of a joint effort by many persons at the Historical Archaeological Experimental Center at Lejre, Denmark (*Historisk-Arkaeologisk Forsøgscenter*). The aim was to learn about the daily life of our ancestors; many of the experiments were carried out specifically to settle moot points that had arisen in archaeological excavations. We have helped each other with the manual labor, we have discussed the agreement between results and theories, and we were often forced to console ourselves with the fact that "a negative result is indeed a result." Above all, we have enjoyed making these primitive experiments, and for this I want to give my warmest thanks to all my volunteer helpers at the Center in Lejre.

I also want to express my gratitude to the Center, to its founders and managers, and to the foundations and institutions that have supported it. The Center has been—and in my opinion will continue to be—of great importance in its experimental work, particularly in giving children and adolescents a knowledge of the simple working methods of the past.

Arne Bjørn

Detail from a scene on a Greek vase from the 6th century: tending the fire in a potter's kiln which is ornamented with a mask.

1 Fire

Sooner or later every boy or girl will experiment with fire. It has been so throughout the generations, and adults have always realized that it would be wisest to join in—and why not? It's fun for everyone, and what is fun and experienced first hand is always remembered better than what is read in a textbook.

At the Historical Archaeological Experimental Center at Lejre, Denmark, we attempt to understand how our ancestors lived, and undeniably fire plays the most significant role in our experiments with life as it was lived in ancient times. Fire is considered man's most important discovery; in northern latitudes it was essential to make living conditions tolerable for our ancestors. It was used outdoors and indoors, by men and by women, for work and for celebrations. Each little child from his first wobbly step on had to learn to be careful of the open fire; this was a natural part of his life.

Today, with central heating and electric ranges, the situation is quite different. One seldom sees a fire in the home any more; yet everyone feels cozy and snug sitting around an open, warming fire and staring into the dancing flames and hot embers. Could this be part of our ancient inheritance, reaching back through many generations to the time our ancestors first sat around a bonfire? No, it is not that in itself. What is indeed inherited is man's, and especially youth's, desire to experiment. Man is never so happy as when he has found out something for himself—he has discovered his working method for himself, and his joy is not diminished even though others discovered the same thing years before.

From the time we are very young, we perceive the world around us and make discoveries that are new to us and form the basis for our experiences. During the first fifteen or so years of life the young will have to absorb society's entire technology, which has taken man two hundred thousand years to develop. It is anything but easy, but it should not be boring. Practical experiments can tell us much about our ancestors' living conditions and give us knowledge and understanding in a completely different way than just reading about it.

Fire has an eternal attraction for those who want to experiment for

Iron Age village at Lejre in 1967. The houses are all reconstructions based on excavations of house sites in Denmark. The interiors are equipped with furniture as they would have been about 2000 years ago. One house was inhabited in 1967. In the gable just under the thatched roof is the louver opening that forms the draft for the open fireplaces in these houses. The half-hidden house in the left foreground was burned down in August 1967 in order to examine the remains and compare them to the remains of ancient houses archaeologists have discovered and thus determine if these reconstructions are accurate.

themselves. Despite our modern technology, even the most primitive working methods with fire are still in use today. This is especially true in warmer climates where the demands for indoor comfort and heating are less important.

Our experiments at Lejre were primarily designed to investigate our own ancestors' primitive working methods and thus to interpret the vestiges and remains that the archaeologists find in their excavations. We wanted to find out how they lived, how they got heat and light, and how they cooked and made their pots and tools. This we could do only through field experiments. All these questions are far from answered as yet, but we have discovered some of the old working methods. They are described in this book so you may try them for yourself and perhaps even carry the experiments further.

The fact that fire is so dangerous to work with is quite a drawback. Aside from simply burning your fingers, if you are not careful the fire will become your master and cause great damage in various ways. Hence in almost every society there are laws and ordinances governing how to work and deal with fire. The laws are based on these ground rules:

Never light a fire near anything flammable. Do it far away from houses, heather, or coniferous trees, since sparks can fly far.

10

School-children tend the firing of one of the old pottery kilns.

Children must never play with fire unless adults participate or supervise.

Never light a bigger fire than you need.

Carefully put out the fire before you leave. Use sand or dirt to kill the last embers.

Never light a fire on someone else's property without the owner's permission.

Never light a fire indoors except in a permanent hearth or fireplace. Even a peaceful candle can cause great damage.

Carbon monoxide and strong smoke from bad fireplaces or partially smothered fires can be dangerous if inhaled. You must never light a fire in a closed room unless there is a regular chimney and good ventilation.

11

Above. *An old Roman potter's kiln from Emperor Augustus' time found at Ledignan (farm) in France. It is built of rough-hewn stone and clay and is much better preserved than the Danish find of the same period. This is partly because it was built of solid material and partly because the climate is much drier in this area.*

A child can easily fire clay in his own open pit after he has helped adults with the work and understands that the fire must be handled carefully and that the kiln must be placed where there is no danger of the fire spreading. (If his mother had noticed that he was about to be photographed, this child would have been given a clean sweater— which would have been unfortunate because that's not natural clothing for pot firing in an open pit.)

Experiments with fire in the Iron Age houses in Lejre show that if the fire accidentally catches on any flammable household objects, you have at the most two minutes to get out of the house. Beyond that time it is perilous to stay in a burning room.

Actually, my own experiments with fire and clay were not started because of an interest in fire as such, but as an investigation of pottery from the Iron Age. During the excavation work for a building project in Glostrup, Denmark, we found some sites of Iron Age houses and potters' kilns. The sites contained an abundance of different types of potsherds. We took on the investigation in order to find out how our Iron Age potters had produced such different types of fired clay bodies

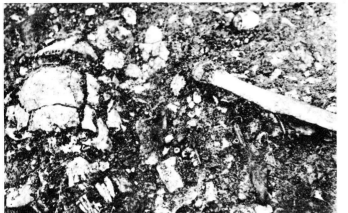

Fire

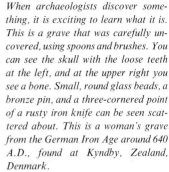

When archaeologists discover something, it is exciting to learn what it is. This is a grave that was carefully uncovered, using spoons and brushes. You can see the skull with the loose teeth at the left, and at the upper right you see a bone. Small, round glass beads, a bronze pin, and a three-cornered point of a rusty iron knife can be seen scattered about. This is a woman's grave from the German Iron Age around 640 A.D., found at Kyndby, Zealand, Denmark.

The find in this picture was difficult to interpret. It contained many clay potsherds from the Celtic Iron Age, around 100 B.C. There was a hole with much charcoal, covered by a fallen layer of fired clay (position marked by matchbox in picture). It must have been a kiln, but unfortunately reconstruction was not possible because of its poor state of preservation. Very little can be seen in a black-and-white photograph: color photographs show the contrast in the character of the earth much more definitely. The find is at Lindholm at Gevning, Zealand, Denmark.

13

Left. *It is clear that this find has something to do with a kiln base. A solid layer of clay has been fired. It is surrounded by clinkers, but we have only the base of the kiln to go by—the rest must be reconstructed. Iron kiln (warming oven?) from the site at Ballerup Church, Zealand.*

Below. *The excavation of the remains of a prehistoric kiln at Sylt in Schleswig —not much more than the colored layer of earth in the sandy subsoil. The type is known from places inhabited by the Lombards, who were very good potters and lived just south of Denmark. The Museum of Schleswig-Holstein, Gottorp, West Germany.*

and pot surfaces and how they used their kilns. And we have come up with some good results. Most significantly, we discovered that you can make usable potters' kilns by such simple methods as mud-and-wattle, and in addition to using these kilns to fire replicas of the black, unglazed pottery of the past, we also discovered that they are in many ways as good as modern kilns.

2 Bonfire

Nothing is known about when man discovered fire. The discovery lies so far back in prehistoric times that we have no exact knowledge of how our oldest progenitors made use of this important element (the ancient Greeks believed the world consisted of four elements: water, fire, earth, and air). We must use our imaginations and place ourselves in the primeval stage of man's evolution to visualize how the primitive hunter and his companions reacted to their first encounter with fire.

Presumably, man first saw and experienced fire during catastrophes of nature, such as a forest fire caused by lightning. A forest fire meant danger, and a race for safety was necessary to avoid being burned or suffocated. Volcanoes were equally dangerous manifestations of nature; their red-hot rocks and flowing lava, thundering explosions, sulfurous vapors, and scalding water were all associated with the phenomenon of fire and were feared.

Men of the past were very probably just as curious as we are today. The unusual, however awesome, had to be investigated and tested, and the story ends with fire being tamed and utilized as one of man's earliest technical aids. *Homo sapiens*, that gifted species, has gained superiority over all other animal species partly because of his ability to master fire.

The bonfire must have been man's first use of fire. Imagine a time when man had neither house nor tent for the night. He had only the heat of a bonfire to give him warmth and comfort, and the circle of light became his zone of security in the dark. It was much like being in a closed room into which no carnivorous animals or supernatural beings dared enter.

Primitive people soon mastered the art of building a good campfire and of tending it; this was pure necessity and in many cases a matter of survival. Regardless of whether you belonged to a band of reindeer hunters thousands of years ago, or were one of Jack London's Alaskan goldminers during our own time, who wanted to turn in for the night, a fire had to be lighted and large branches and small twigs had to be gathered to light and feed the fire. A suitable site had to be found,

Bonfire with shelter and perhaps some large rocks available to make a ring around the fire. Preparations are necessary in order to light a fire. It is futile to light a few twigs and then, as the fire dies down, dash about the neighbourhood to look for firewood. All that should be done before lighting the fire. The old reindeer hunters knew it was impossible to hunt for firewood in the middle of the night, if they had gathered too little, and they also knew that a great deal of trouble could result if the fire spread through heather or other flammable material that had not been cleared from the area around the bonfire.

The fire tender was an important person among primitive hunters, since he understood this dangerous element. A skilled tender often appeared almost supernatural in the eyes of his companions; he had a covenant with the god of fire and he always knew how the fire should be laid, a most important matter, since each type of fire served its own special purpose.

This is a large pagoda fire. Built of thin tree trunks or thick branches placed in an open square one above the other. It is lighted by setting fire to the pile of dry grass and twigs placed inside the pagoda. This is an effective bonfire that provides much light and heat. The form can be used for large and small bonfires.

An occasional small fire during a short stop on a hike is best and most easily laid as a star fire or Indian fire. Find a large tuft of dry grass, a couple of handfuls of dry twigs, and well over a dozen thick poles or sticks about 2 feet long. Press the dry grass together and place it in the middle of the area for the fire. Place the twigs on top, then the sticks, with one end over the middle of the fire so that it will look like a star when seen from above. When the pressed grass is lighted the twigs will catch fire and their flames in turn will heat the thicker poles above, which ultimately catch fire. Flames consist of burning gases formed by heating grass, wood, or any flammable material. Straw, paper, and twigs are the most easily heated to produce combustible gases, hence these materials are used for kindling. They burn out fast, however, and therefore you can only hope that the heat from them is intense enough to initiate the gas production and make the thicker sticks catch fire.

Bonfire

This fire here is made of parallel logs on the hearth of an Iron Age house. The fire doesn't flame much, but it makes a great deal of charcoal, which holds the heat for a long time.

Bonfire

The largest gas emanation from a heated piece of wood always comes from the end, because the grain of the wood runs longitudinally and conducts the gas through the stick. Therefore the sticks have to be laid with one end in the middle of the fire. The thick sticks produce charcoal as the wood is consumed, and since the charcoal forms an intensely hot layer of embers you can keep pushing the sticks farther and farther in toward the center until it is time to put out the fire or replenish it.

Sometimes a fast-burning fire with strong, high flames is needed. For this everything must burst into flames at once. The kind of fire to build is the pyramid or wigwam fire, where the heavy wood logs are placed standing in teepee fashion around plenty—and that means *plenty*—of absolutely dry kindling wood. Finally, you can add some

A stone-encircled fireplace built in the open. A few large stones will keep the live coals from flying around and will act as a support for a grill or kettle. Here plants are being cooked to provide dye for yarn for hand weaving at Lejre.

Star-shaped fire.

Pyramid fire.

Bonfire

Beacon fire with high flames, fed with straw and evergreen branches. This fire gives an enormous light that can be seen from far off, but it does not last long. The sparks fly a considerable distance in the wind.

Bonfire   of the damp or fresh wood if you have any around that you want to use up.

This is the most common form for the beacon bonfires that have been used for generations as signal fires or for festive bonfires, such as Midsummer Night and on Saint Hans' Evening, June 23, in Denmark. It is without doubt the best-known type of bonfire in modern Denmark, and in America it is popular on Hallowe'en. Most of us have surely seen such a bonfire with its upward surging blaze sending sparks into the black sky. We have seen how far the sparks soar, especially when a wind is up. The sight is truly beautiful, but it is dangerous if houses or haystacks are within reach.

The best fire for concentrated heat, for cooking, for example, is one made with closely laid parallel logs, sometimes called a hunter or pioneer lay. The fire is raised somewhat above the ground by means of a pair of parallel logs set at right angles to the fire logs. The kindling is placed underneath the fuel and lighted there. It may be difficult to ignite this fire if the sticks are too thick, so naturally you should place the thinnest sticks at the bottom. Once the fire is lit and the flames have settled down you have a splendid household fire. The closely set logs keep the fire nourished and they reinforce each other's heat production, concentrating and multiplying the heat. A single log may simply glow too slowly to give any significant heat and most likely will go out; for heat and a good, stable fire, the sticks must lie close together.

Parallel fire.

The parallel fire furnishes an excellent bed of hot charcoal when the wood has burned down. Such a bed of red-hot embers is fine for a later fire. By adding a dry stick now and then the fire can be maintained with low flames for a long time. This was exactly what was wanted for the fire in the open fireplaces of the flammable Iron Age houses, with their thatched roofs directly above the hearths.

You can also make a parallel fire in a trench dug into the ground. This fire holds together better and there is less risk that wind will blow the embers about. Boy Scouts and soldiers often cook over a trench fire; being sheltered from the wind, it provides more concentrated heat. A pair or so of iron rods can be placed across the trench as support for cooking utensils.

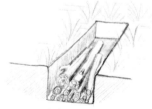

Trench fire.

Of course the very large fire, the council fire, needs more wood. If you have the wood and if the fire must last for a certain length of time and have a certain intensity, the fire should be built in a pagoda shape: large, thick logs laid in a rectangular tower shape. The logs must be placed perfectly horizontal and the longest logs must be at the bottom. During the building, throw sticks and brushwood into the tower and press or stamp them well together. It not only looks best when the pagoda is built as straight and evenly as possible, but it also lessens the danger of its tipping over while burning. To light it, take

Pagoda fire.

20

a large bunch of straw, press it into the kindling at the windward side and light it. If the wood is dry (at least the kindling inside the pagoda must be completely dry) you can get a strong, warming, and high-blazing bonfire that will burn for a long time.

You can make fires in many other ways than those mentioned here. You can use other fuel than wood, but wood was about the only material available to our ancestors, except for peat. Peat, however, is very difficult to get today.

Avoid the use of highly flammable materials such as gasoline (petrol) and kerosene (paraffin). They are very dangerous. Further-more, these flammable liquids have nothing to do with fires of former times. Vapors from these combustible materials can explode if they are poured on a half-doused fire, and if gasoline or kerosene spills on your clothing they may ignite if you come close to the fire. Not only that, but fires started with these materials blaze too violently and create a tremendous amount of smoke; kerosene and gasoline are for lamps, oil furnaces, and engines, where the burning or combustion is under control. Surely no one would think of lighting a fireplace with kerosene; at any rate, you would only do it once, because, in addition to the risk, the mess made by the smoke and soot will require an enormous effort to clean up.

Today we use matches to light a fire, but matches have been known

Here is the fire experiment at Lejre in 1967. An Iron Age house burned to the ground in sixteen minutes, after a fictitious accident on the hearth.

Above right. *Lugged beakers from the Dolmen period. Beakers of this type are found in many types in graves especially in Zealand. Archaeologists have established that they belong to the dolmen period, but we don't know what they were used for. They may have been used to transport charcoal from house to house, or by hunters or shepherds to carry live coals to their campsites.*

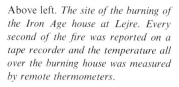

Above left. *The site of the burning of the Iron Age house at Lejre. Every second of the fire was reported on a tape recorder and the temperature all over the burning house was measured by remote thermometers.*

for only about 150 years. We do not know how ancient hunters ignited their fires. Perhaps they "found" fire and brought it home from a nature-ignited fire. Or they may have learned to use a fire drill and bow as the Eskimos have done up to present times. Perhaps they discovered that certain minerals such as flint and iron pyrites create sparks when struck against each other. Only one thing is certain—it was difficult and time-consuming to obtain fire, and therefore the duty of the fire tender was of great importance. The hot charcoal embers in the ashes in the fireplace had to be kept alive during the night in order to start up the fire by blowing on them the next morning. In those days, if one's own fire went out by bad luck, live coals would have to be borrowed from a neighbor. Live coals were transported from place to place, between houses, and on the tribe's wanderings, probably carried in clay pots and later in metal braziers.

Now it is not necessary to be concerned with these difficulties, but it is interesting to imagine how one would have handled the problems of using fire if he had lived 5000 years ago. Possibly one would invent a torch or a lamp for the transport of fire, and the ancients very probably tried that, but we just don't know.

3 Heating

Now, as in the past, fire remains the universal source for heating dwellings. In earlier times, before fire, tribes in the temperate and northern parts of the world built wind-screens, and later houses, as protection from inclement weather, if they were not fortunate enough to find an available cave in their hunting area. Although it was a step forward to have shelter from snow and rain, it could still be bitterly cold inside the cave or house during the winter.

Man's experiences had taught him that fire gave off heat, so, without question, fire had to be brought into the dwelling. How to do this was a real problem, which, of course, was solved by our ancestors all over the world, but not in the same way everywhere.

Today one can simply call a heating expert to find out which heating system is best suited for his own home, but when man first moved fire into a thatched house, he risked burning down the entire house unless he proceeded with the greatest of care. He had to restrict himself to a small, spark-free fire. It probably gave off only radiant heat and also produced an abundance of smoke, making it almost impossible to stay indoors. Yet man solved this problem, too; he devised fireplaces and louver openings and got the heating process organized.

Archaeologists have discovered ancient house sites with fireplaces and ovens. At Lejre, experiments with the Iron Age houses have shown that they could easily have had a good heating-fire on the floor in the middle of a thatched dwelling. For such a fire there must be air holes at both gables up under the apex of the roof. The smoke rises and stays in "layers" under the roof and is sucked out of the louver opening on the lee side. The house must be a certain size, because the distance between the hearth and walls should be $6\frac{1}{2}$ to 10 feet and the distance from the fire to the roof must be 10 to 13 feet. The fire must never have flames higher than 20 inches, and it must never throw sparks up under the roof—but of course our ancestors found out all this for themselves.

One mustn't use straw, paper, or branches for a fire in the hearth. The best material is hot charcoal and 2- to 4-inch-thick branches from hardwood trees stacked for a parallel or hunter's fire. Only a single

Heating

Hearth in Iron Age house. This fire must be tended carefully because of the flammable walls and roof. The best fire is red-hot tree knots.

piece of wood should be added at a time, and just often enough to maintain a good layer of hot charcoal in the hearth. In our ancestors' time, the householder raked the ashes over the embers to bank the fire at night or cautiously pushed the entire fire into an ember pit in the floor close to the hearth. Then he could simply blow on the embers to start up a new fire the next morning.

It was primitive, it was risky, but one thing was certain: everyone knew that fire had to be guarded and treated correctly. Fire was not a toy; it belonged in the hearth or in the oven. It was vital for the well-being of the family, but it could also cause misery and sometimes tragedy.

However, the fire in the hearth was not sufficient to heat the entire house during the winter. One can imagine, therefore, that the inhabitants soon started to use ovens. We know this because we often find the remains of ovens at excavated sites from the Iron Age.

The finest, circular clay-and-wattle ovens with 4- to 8-inch-thick walls have been found. It is uncertain how high these ovens were and whether they had chimneys. Although ovens with remnants of clay chimneys have been found among artifacts of middle-European peoples, no similar ovens have been found in Denmark.

Modern experiments with the primitive oven indicate that a chimney isn't really necessary in a large house with good ventilation. The wood inside the oven burns very well when one tends the fire carefully, although it smokes a bit when the fire is started. When the fuel inside the oven has caught and a layer of hot charcoal has gradually formed at the bottom, it is easy to keep the oven warm day and night by tending it evenly. In fact, it may get so hot that clothing or furs placed there to dry are ignited by the surface heat.

Strangely enough, we haven't definitely found a method of interior heating for the Iron Age other than the hearth and circular oven, but it is clear that Iron Age man experimented with various heating systems. At the Iron Age settlement in Glostrup, Denmark, and later at Jerslev in Hjørring County, Denmark, there were deep-seated, stone-lined fireplaces with long heating-canals out to the sides. The canals were from 16 to 32 inches deep and were covered with a vaulted roof of clay, wholly or partially fired into tile.

Such a canal may have given good heating under the floor of a hut or in a more specialized building such as a grain-drying room or a malt-house. Beer was already known at that time, 2000 years ago, and of course brewing took place all year round. We will just have to guess how they produced the malt for the beer during the cold months, but to do so they had to have some kind of heating system.

Much later our Nordic ancestors acquired the art of writing, which enabled them to leave written testimony about their life and activities. Among the first written accounts of interior heating, we find some by Saxo Grammaticus, who, in the thirteenth century, tells the story of how King Rolf and his men were almost burned to death at a feast because of a long hearth (*langbaal*) in the banquet hall. This incident took place many hundreds of years before it was recorded, probably around the year 500.

In the early Viking Period long hearths started to appear in the main rooms. Presumably this occurred at the same time as the construction of more exclusive timber houses with dressed plank ceilings, for these ceilings were less flammable than thatched roofs. Long hearths have been found at sites from the Viking Period in Iceland, Ireland, and on the Shetland Islands, and, judging from the sagas, they must have also been known in Denmark.

The Vikings learned and saw much on their "study trips" abroad. If they had not already known the brazier with charcoal fire in

Hearth fire and clay cooking pots in an Iron Age house. This picture was taken during winter experiments in 1967, when the house was lived in for a whole month. To measure the temperature, thermometers were hung in various locations in the house.

Denmark, that must have been one of the good innovations the Vikings brought home with them, because the first known braziers of baked clay stem from the late Viking Period.

This method of heating was almost forgotten until it became fashionable some years ago to have a charcoal brazier or grill in the backyard. Outdoors, that is most sensible. Indoors, the grill should only be used on a stone floor and in a place with excellent ventilation, such as a chimney flue or louvered opening in the ceiling or roof. If a grill with a charcoal fire is used in a small, closed room, carbon monoxide is produced, which, of course, is poisonous if inhaled.

A charcoal grill is easy to ignite: place a few hot coals from an oven or fireplace into the charcoal, blow, and watch the flames leap up. Pieces of charcoal made by charcoal burners are dry and easy to light. A little charcoal lighter can be used to start the fire in a modern grill, but it must never be used if the grill is hot or if hot coals are present, as the fluid may explode. *Never* use kerosene (paraffin) as it smokes and makes the grill smell for a very long time. It is better to use pieces of thin paper under the charcoal even if these do smoke a bit at first.

The fireplace has existed in Scandinavia ever since the Viking Period, but this was mostly in the large houses of the well-to-do. It only came into more extensive use after the monks had introduced the art of building chimneys out of burnt lime and bricks. Far into the Middle Ages, the common man had to manage with hearth and brazier.

Little by little, peasants and townspeople saw chimneys on the monasteries and manor houses, and they decided that the farmhouse and the village house had to be improved. So chimneys were built with a brick smoke cap and a pair of side walls to form a hooded space for firing. All activities requiring fire were carried out in the hooded opening under the chimney. Here was the hearth for cooking, the copper laundry kettle, and if there was a baking oven and a malt kiln for drying sprouted barley, they were there, too, and they shared a common air shaft to the hood. It was practical and it diminished the danger of fire accidents, but the heat did not get into the room. The general population had no money for a chimney-with-a-fireplace, and so it was never widespread in Denmark. Instead, a jamb stove, that is a stove fed from another room was developed. In the beginning this was simply a stove built of bricks as a hump into the room from the kitchen hearth. From the kitchen one could push embers and fuel into the hump stove. All smoke and fumes went back and up the chimney hood.

This gave a little more warmth in the room, but a brick stove doesn't give off much heat because its walls are too thick. Therefore, special stove bricks were made: bowl-shaped tiles (*kakler*) of hard fired clay. They were thinner and allowed better heat transfer. Normally the tiles were glazed on the outside, and for the more select stoves the tiles were

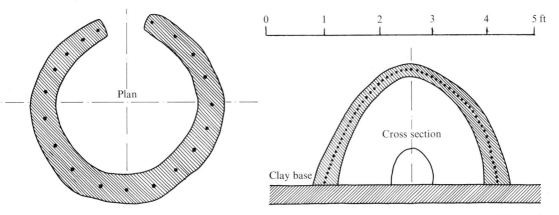

Plan

Cross section

Clay base

0   1   2   3   4   5 ft

Dome-shaped oven built of clay-and-wattle. This comes from an Iron Age house in Sortemuld on the island of Bornholm.

Pots and hearth in an Iron Age house. Charcoal embers and ashes lie in an even layer, ready for food preparation.

Heating

A boy firing a dome-shaped oven in an Iron Age house. Dry evergreen branches and straw are used and it smokes a great deal in the beginning. When the fire has caught and flamed up, an even fire can be attained with dry branches and charcoal and kept as a smoke-free, warm, even fire night and day. A chimney is not necessary, and carbon monoxide is not formed as long as the fire hole is kept open.

covered with pressed relief designs. The walls around the stove were decorated with painted tiles.

It was not until the seventeenth century that jamb stoves made of cast iron became common, and at that time free-standing cast-iron stoves for heating rooms also started to appear. The smoke from the detached stoves went through a stove pipe to a chimney in the same room. Certain conditions permitted several stoves to vent to the same chimney as long as the chimney drew well enough to prevent smoke from getting into the room. All the detached stoves inherited the name tile stove (*kakkelovn*) from the oldest type, even though the new ones were made of iron, not tile.

Only fifty years ago almost every home used coal- or wood-burning stoves, and everyone knew how to deal with fire in the home. Today many persons, perhaps most, have never tried to start up a stove, but it is interesting and worth the effort to try if the opportunity comes along. You can learn a great deal about fire from such an experience.

Today the dream of many families is to have a fireplace in the living room. There are two main types of fireplaces; one is an open fireplace in the wall (*kamin*) usually made of brick walls built into the chimney, the other (*pejs*) is extended from one or two walls and is usually built of stone with a hood leading into a chimney.

It is a pity to leave a fireplace unused, either because you don't want to take the time to set it up and light it or because it is too difficult to light without having it smoke. Try, instead, to learn about it thoroughly. Most commonly one would build a parallel fire on a pair of andirons or an iron gate. However, many fireplaces give the best fire when the fuel—preferably long pieces—is placed vertically in a wigwam formation, perhaps in the corner of the fireplace. Underneath and behind put lots of crumpled newspaper. At least two or three newspapers are needed to supply the high flames necessary to heat the chimney quickly. Then it will draw well, so flames and smoke are sucked up into the chimney along the path of the wood. Now and then

Two jamb stoves seen from the living room. Notice that there are no doors on these stoves. They are fired from the kitchen, which is behind the white wall. Laesøgaarden (farm), Open Air Museum, Lyngby, Denmark.

29

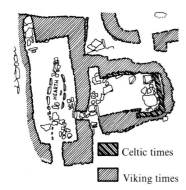

■ Celtic times

▨ Viking times

Diagram of house remains from Viking times, excavated on the Shetland Islands. In the middle of the room are the remains of the stone-lined long hearth.

the fire must be pushed closely together and fed before it burns down.

Birch and beech burn best; they both produce quiet flames without sparks and each has its own distinctive scent. Ash catches and burns quickly. Oak burns slowly, so the fire often goes out. It is dangerous to burn evergreens in a fireplace without a firescreen; the high resin content in evergreens results in a gas production that causes explosions in the wood and these in turn hurl sparks great distances.

A fire in the fireplace or stove renews the air in a room. There is a continuous circulation of fresh air because the fire uses the air in the room and sends it up the chimney while fresh new air is drawn in through cracks at the windows and doors. That's just one of the advantages of having "living" fire in your house.

4 Fire for Cooking

Can you imagine eating raw food? Yes, perhaps raw vegetables and fruit, but not raw fish or raw meat. We can quickly agree that in food preparation the use of fire has greatly improved man's lot. Not only does food taste better when it is cooked, although it may be just a habit to think so, but it is also healthier, easier to digest, and free from dangerous bacteria that must have plagued our ancestors with illness and death. Most bacteria cannot tolerate heat above 167 °F.

Primitive people did not realize this, but they undoubtedly discovered that meat and fish had more flavour and were more tender when roasted or boiled than when eaten raw. Cooked porridge and baked bread, too, were easier and pleasanter to eat than raw grain.

Since all the known methods of food preparation—roasting, boiling, smoking, baking—were discovered thousands of years ago and later refined and improved, it will be interesting to find out how it all started. It is also a worthwhile and agreeable experiment, since simple food often tastes best.

Cooking on a spit or grill has become fashionable, but it is nothing new. In fact, this is probably the oldest method of preparing food man has known. Put a piece of meat on a spit and hold it over a charcoal fire. It is absurdly easy to do. After a few tries and a little instruction, such as basting the meat with melted shortening or vegetable oil, one can easily discover how much cooking a steak or chicken needs. The nice thing about it is that the meat retains its true flavour. There is no fattening gravy and no spice to cover up the true taste. If, out of habit, you believe that meat requires spices, you can always add them later, even though cook-book authors tell you that spices should be added before cooking.

The grill (outdoor grill) can be made in many ways. One can buy expensive, and excellent, grills, but since we are trying to do it primitively the materials we need will not be expensive. We'll make the kind of grill we see used today in Sardinia and other Mediterranean islands.

Find an old, discarded iron wash basin, collect ten to twenty pieces of dry wood, put them in the wash basin and set fire to them. In half an hour the wood will become hot charcoal, which should fill the basin.

31

A pointed stick is the oldest method of cooking over fire.

If there is not enough, put more wood on the fire and let it burn. As soon as the flames and smoke stop, the "brazier," covered with a spit or a grate is ready for cooking. In the south of Europe it is the husband's duty to get the brazier ready for use in the course of the morning, so his wife can prepare dinner. If things aren't in order there will be an argument that all the neighbors can hear, since the brazier stands on the steps outside the front door, or in the street.

If one wants to cook soup in a primitive yet modern way, put a piece of drain pipe on its end in the middle of the brazier and put the soup pot on top, close to the hot coals. If you want to grill steaks, put a heavy iron grate over the coals; this improvised grill works beautifully. If you buy charcoal, it's easier of course. Then all you need do is fill your basin-grill with charcoal, pour on some charcoal lighter, and light it. The charcoal will be ready to use shortly. One can use a variety of grates on the grill: an old stove grate, a drain grating, or even pieces of round iron. If you've seen cooking in the small Mediterranean villages you won't be surprised by any of these.

We know that in Denmark it often happens that archaeological excavations uncover stone-built fire pits. They were fireplaces from celebrations where an entire suckling pig, lamb, deer, or several geese were roasted. Today one can enjoy such a fireplace in his own back

Old fashioned Viking Period cooking vessel hangs over the fire by a rope protected by "swallow's nest" (svale-reder) projections, seen clearly as knobs on the rim of the vessel at the left of the picture. A little pot containing meat and hot charcoal stands at the edge of the fire.

Food in preparation placed on the hearth in an Iron Age house; the fire has to be flamed up. A clay pot is placed on clay andirons; the holes in the andirons are for inserting a stick to remove them while they are hot.

Fire for Cooking

Left. *Interior of a Spanish country kitchen. Here cooking is still done over an open fire on a stone floor. Talayots, Mallorca.*

Right. *The Spanish peasant still makes food in a clay pot over a little fire on a stone floor. It takes a bit longer to cook soup this way, but it also tastes better. Talayots, Mallorca.*

yard. A fire pit is usually about 20 inches deep, 48 inches long, and 24 inches wide. Put two or three layers of fist-sized stones on the bottom for a rack and set a couple of sod blocks at each end to direct the draft through the stone layer and in under the fire. In the middle, put the wood and use a bit of straw or bark for kindling, unless you "cheat" and use paper. While the flames burn down, hunt for half a dozen flat stones (not flint) and place these on the bed of hot coals. When the fire has burned halfway down, position the stones so they are as level as possible. If you have figured the wood accurately and have obtained the correct layer of coals, you will have a bed of red-hot stones in half an hour. Then you can roast your meat or do other cooking for about three or four hours. If you permit "cheating," you could wrap the meat in aluminum foil. Fish is excellent cooked in this way. Primitive tribes on Borneo even today use this type of fireplace, normally wrapping the meat in large leaves.

The fire pit is inexpensive to make: some stones and a hole in the ground and half a dozen sod blocks are all it takes. There is nothing costly to buy. You must just remember to make it as far away from the house as possible—and certainly not anywhere near a thatched roof.

The baking oven was also an early discovery. In its simplest form it is just a hole dug about 3 feet down into the ground, with a height and width of about 1½ feet. Make a very intense fire in the hole, and when it has burned down, rake out remaining coals and ashes. Now you can put the bread into the hot "oven." Cover the hole with a couple of rocks. Such primitive baking is done to this day in South America. This type of oven, however, is not advisable for areas where the soil is too loose and sandy. Such soil is too moist and requires considerable heat to dry it out. In such areas it is better to use an Iron Age dome-shaped oven. This is an ideal oven to build at a scout camp or at a summer cottage. It is excellent for baking and cooking, as is obvious from its use in many Italian and southern French *pizzarias*.

A good tasting pizza is easy to make. Mix three cups of flour, a bit of salt, a pinch of sugar and baking powder together in a bowl. Add about one tablespoon of vegetable oil and then carefully add as much water as necessary to knead it into a firm dough the consistency of potter's clay. Roll out a handful of dough as thin as possible and bend the edges up. It is best to put it on a greased metal sheet, because this makes it easier to put on the juicy, cut tomatoes, tomato purée,

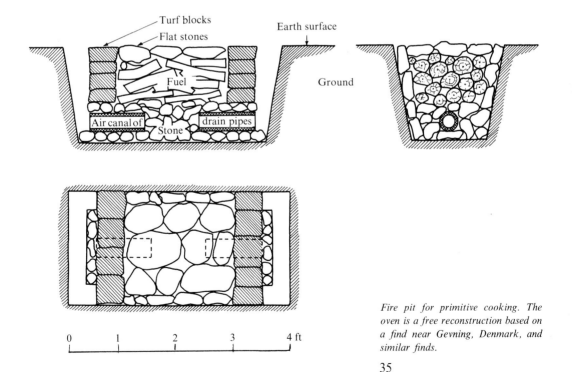

Fire pit for primitive cooking. The oven is a free reconstruction based on a find near Gevning, Denmark, and similar finds.

35

anchovies, black olives, and fresh or smoked meat topping. Everything must be ready because it must bake fast. Finally pour a little oil over the pizza and push the entire pizza into the oven, using a long-handled wooden paddle. Bake three to four minutes. You can make other things, such as apple pie, in the same way, but here we will only describe the procedure.

After two hours of pre-firing, the oven is normally hot enough and it is only necessary to replenish the fire with a piece of wood now and then. To bake pizza, pie, or cake, push the coals over to one side of the oven, and put the pastry on the other side. You can get especially fine baking and roasting results in such a superheated oven. For grilling, rake some coals toward the front and place a heavy iron grate on top. In a short time it will be hot enough to grill a most delicious steak.

It's great fun to watch an Italian chef handle his pizza oven: two or three pizzas in and out of the oven, steaks on the grill, and just inside the oven opening a clay pot with soup simmering gently.

Our ancestors weren't able to make soup until the pot was invented. This happened in the Stone Age, despite the lack of bronze and iron. Wooden bowls were, of course out of the question—unless they dis-

Complete oven from Varese, Corsica, for baking or cooking. In Mediterranean lands the climate is so equable that nearly all ovens are built outdoors. A clay soup pot stands inside the oven, left over from the last meal. This large oven is fired only now and then, but it is used for all kinds of food preparation.

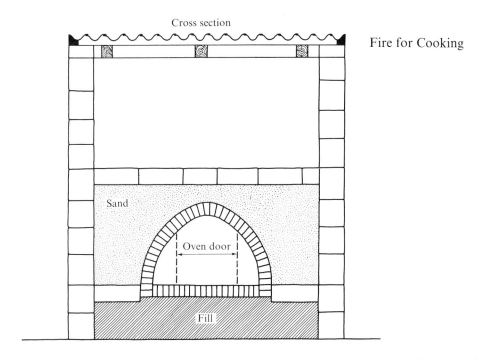

Cross section

Fire for Cooking

Sand

Oven door

Fill

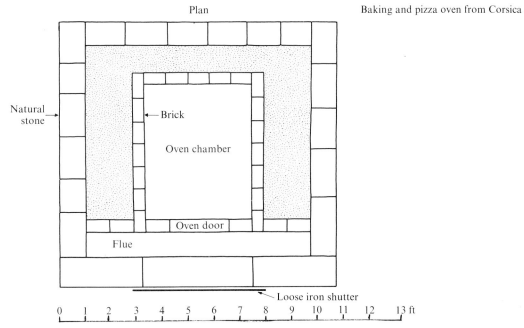

Plan

Baking and pizza oven from Corsica

Natural
stone

Brick

Oven chamber

Oven door

Flue

Loose iron shutter

0   1   2   3   4   5   6   7   8   9   10   11   12   13 ft

Fire for Cooking

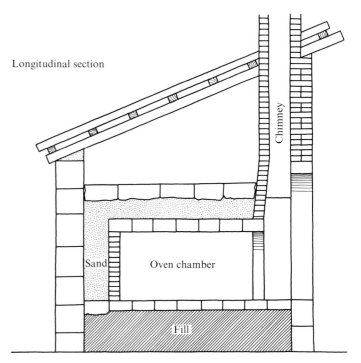

Longitudinal section

Chimney

Sand

Oven chamber

Fill

covered that you could drop red-hot stones into the soup until it boiled. That would not make a very good soup according to our taste. Of course, a few may have been lucky enough to find a soft variety of stone, such as soapstone, which could be hollowed out to form a cooking utensil. However, since this type of stone is rare outside certain mountainous areas, clay pots became the cooking utensils. Primitive people discovered that clay could be fired to become a hard, stone-like material. Then one taught the other that if you took clay and wedged it and added powdered calcined granite, you could form a clay pot. If this pot were put into the fire or maybe even into a dome-shaped oven, and baked hot, it would become a fine cooking pot.

In southern Europe as well as in many primitive countries people still use clay cooking pots today. They are home-manufactured and inexpensive. In Denmark, the Jutland women (*jydepottekoner*) made most of the cooking utensils used by the peasants, villagers, and the townspeople, over open fireplaces in the old kitchens. These cooking vessels are called Jutland pots (*jydepotter*).

Fire for Cooking

Old baking oven from Kalvehave, Denmark, built of large unfired bricks stuck together with a clay mortar. The oven is built outdoors, but a fire opening is made into the scullery wall. It was insulated with gravel.

Two common cooking vessels of biscuit-fired clay with inside surfaces glazed in brown lead-glaze. Such vessels are made and sold inexpensively and used daily in the Spanish countryside.

Jutland pot, the Danish cooking pot in use for hundreds of years.

Two frying pans of brown glazed clay. Mallorca 1967.

Given enough time, it is actually better to make soup and porridge in clay rather than in metal pots, since slow heating up and long simmering make the best soup and gruel. There are, however, few housewives nowadays who have that much time for cooking. But just imagine the upheaval in the old-time kitchens when iron pots and copper kettles replaced clay or Jutland pots. Many an old grandmother must have shaken her head in disapproval of these modern methods.

Fire for Cooking

A Jutland pot is being scraped and polished so that the clay attains a firm, smooth surface. The pot is hard-fired without a glaze, and has been used as a cooking pot right up to the present day.

5 Clay

Everyone who lives in low-lying country knows what clay is. It is found almost everywhere in the ground. If a good place has been found it can very often be dug up and used directly as it is, including the sand, gravel, and other impurities that might be present. This type of clay, however, can be used only for mud-built or clay-built houses and primitive ovens. These structures make little demand on the clay, so almost any type of clay can be used. If, on the other hand, the clay is to be used for pottery, you must have a fat, plastic type of clay very rarely found in nature. You may find it, of course, but only in a few places and usually not close at hand. As a rule, in Denmark the old method of making Jutland pots as a cottage industry on farms developed because a bed of fine micaceous clay existed close to the farmhouse.

In the fall the farmer would bring home two or three loads of clay from the local clay pit. The clay was spread out on a stone floor in the scullery or barn, where it was kneaded with bare feet, by the women and girls. They had to stamp out all the clods in the clay, and during the kneading they added water until the clay attained the right consistency. Then it was shoveled into a corner, where it remained in a massive heap for use throughout the winter. Usually the clay was so fat that they had to add 25 to 50 per cent of fine sand or silver sand before use. If potter's clay is too fat, it will be too soft to form large pots; they will sag and get a "pot belly" or split when they are left to dry. Pure clay in its plastic state lacks rigidity. Potter's clay must be stable, or the form will collapse. Adding sand to clay makes it firmer because the inner friction between the mineral grains in the clay increases and prevents it from flowing.

The potters of old understood this problem, and therefore mixed in fine sand—not coarse sand, since this would cause streaks in the surface later, during the polishing and burnishing. In addition, there is the danger that some of the larger mineral grains might not be fire-proof but would expand or explode during the firing, which would result in a splitting off of large chips or would create pockmarks in the surface. One could heat the coarse sand red-hot, in an old cracked

Clay

Clay can be used to make a very complex firing place into a kiln. When the clay has dried and been fired to tile, the kiln can be used for many firings.

pot, before use, but our ancestors very likely used powdered, calcined granite as an aggregate in the clay for their larger pots. It can be clearly seen in the potsherds from ancient times that the body of the clay was strengthened with sharp-edged mineral grains that can be obtained only from crushed, fired rock—grains of sand are rounded by wear from the movements of water or the wash of waves.

Clay can be tested to see if it is suitable for making into a pot by taking a small lump and rolling it into $\frac{3}{4}$-inch coil and bending it into a ring of about 2 inches inside diameter. The clay must not split and the ring must be so firm that it can be set on its edge without sagging. If the clay splits, it is too lean or perhaps only too dry. The latter may be helped by kneading the clay with more water. If the ring sags, the clay lacks rigidity, and this may be caused by either too much water or too little sand.

These tests may seem to be something of a nuisance in the beginning, but it seldom takes long for even novices to get a feel for how best to work with the clay. And besides, each and every potter puts his special demands on the clay and prepares it in his own way.

The potters of 2000 years ago prepared their clay in pits in the ground. They dug a hollow approximately 30 inches in diameter and

43

20 inches deep. They filled this with clay (almost always blue clay), which they then mixed and stamped until it presumably became very thin. Then they added some wood ash, as can be seen by the presence of small particles of charcoal in the clay pits that have been discovered. Large pebbles in the clay were sorted out, while smaller pebbles and gravel were allowed to remain and settle in the mixed mass of clay. When the clay was sufficiently mixed, the clay pit was covered with soil. The clay matured there while the excess water seeped out into the soil until the clay obtained the right consistency. Clay will keep like this for hundreds of years. At the Center in Lejre we have made pots from clay found prepared in pits at the excavation of the potter's kiln in Glostrup.

Wood ash contains potash (potassium carbonate), which affects the clay chemically and renders it more plastic. It also lowers the temperature to which the clay must be heated in order to vitrify it; thus it is possible to fire hard-baked clay pots at somewhat lower temperatures.

This explains the presence of the ash. On the other hand, ritual is our only explanation for the presence of the body of a cow in the bottom of the clay pits discovered at sites prior to the excavation at Glostrup. We can suppose that the local heathen priest or guild master solemnly dedicated the clay pit during a special ceremony by putting in the body and at the same time spreading some wood ash over it, which improved the clay. Superstition, habit, ignorance, secret methods, and the like made clay preparation cumbersome. Even today it is very easy to get into an argument with a potter by meddling in the making of his particular clay body. For our experiments it is not that important to be able to prepare the clay ourselves. We can buy it ready made: washed, wedged, shaped into big loaves, and wrapped tightly in plastic to retain its moisture for a long time.

Novices do not immediately discover the problems in working with clay. As you handle a lump of clay that is delightful to knead and shape into all sorts of objects, all the marvellous possibilities of ceramics begin to stir in your imagination.

But everything must have a beginning, so it is wisest to start your experimentation with small things until you understand the clay and its limitations as well as its possibilities. Start out, for instance, with small candleholders and ashtrays. Make several of each until you can make such bowl or cup shapes without fingerprints and without splitting them. Also practice achieving a uniform thickness on the bottom. Remember for modelling one must always *squeeze* the clay into shape, never pull it, or else small splits will show up when the objects are fired.

When we tackle somewhat larger things we follow a method that will never be out-dated, even though it's the most primitive method

Clay

Clay can be kneaded best with bare feet—when no machine is available. It is effective, but you get very dirty. However, it is easy to wash clay off, and it actually cleans the skin.

known—the finger or pinching method, or Jutland pot method. Despite the use of the potter's wheel for many centuries, this modelling method has remained in use from ancient times to today, and it has been used to create the most beautiful pottery ever made.

Small things such as cups, bowls, and candlesticks are formed from a cylinder of well-kneaded clay about 2 by 2 inches. Put this on its base and start to hollow it out by pushing both thumbs down into the center. Then squeeze and pinch it into the desired form. Do it cautiously. The clay is a living mass that must be caressed with small gentle squeezes and pinches to make the walls an even thickness everywhere and the surface attractively smooth.

45

Clay

A little clay pot is easy to shape using only your fingers, but it takes great care to get the surface nice and smooth. The girl seems to be succeeding here, even though she is a beginner.

The genuine, large Jutland pots, as mentioned before, originated in Jutland, Denmark, and are related to the ancient black pots found at excavations. They were made by women at home, who specialized in this work; they have supplied large parts of the country with crocks, cooking vessels, and pans even up to the present. These pots were formed from a well-kneaded loaf or *kat* of clay, 6 to 8 inches long and 4 inches in diameter. To start making such a pot, use a square wooden board 12 by 12 inches on your lap as an aid, as the potter women did. Also have on hand a small pail or pot of water and an old cup filled with slip (clay suspended in water). Smear a little of the thin slip on the middle of your board as lubrication, then on top of that put the clay *kat*, on its narrow end. To hollow out the lump, start with your thumbs and later press with your fist. It is essential to keep the wall evenly thick at all times, so the hollow must be right in the center. While you work keep turning the pot around on the board. Don't let the clay get too dry. Have a wet cloth ready, soaked in slip and folded once or twice. Use it for moistening and smoothing the surface as well as to form the lip. As you press the walls thin, always push against the outer side with your free hand while you press from the inside ("squeeze"), otherwise the pot will split. If the clay is too moist it is often necessary to let the pot rest several hours before finishing. The

46

walls must be less than $\frac{3}{8}$ inch in thickness, but not less than $\frac{3}{16}$ inch.

If the wall or edge splits during the shaping, repair it with slip. It is best to use the upper layer of slip that has formed in the vessel used for washing the clay. Better yet, try to avoid splitting in the first place.

After shaping, let the clay pot dry two or three days until the clay becomes leather hard. Then polish and scrape the surface by rubbing with a smooth flat stone, the rib of a hog or sheep, or with the back of a big spoon. This produces a shine on the surface of your Jutland pot. In this way you can also make patterns on the pot, as was often done. Set the pot aside for drying, preferably for a full month. The pot will crack if the initial drying is too fast. First place it in a shed where the air is somewhat humid; later place it in a centrally heated basement. The old potter women often gave their pots a final drying on iron rods over the hearth, so they became slightly smoked or sooted at the same time.

Another primitive method of the past is the building up of clay pots by coils. This is by far the oldest known method in Denmark. It is particularly suited for use with rather lean clay for making somewhat heavier and thicker-walled clay pots.

Start out with the bottom of the pot. Make a base disc of the size and shape you want for the bottom of the pot by forming a ball of clay, flattening it with the palm of your hand, and cutting it to size. Then make a coil as long as the circumference of the bottom and about $\frac{3}{4}$ inch thick. Press the coil a bit flat and put it on top of the disc as a ring along the outer edge. Push it down firmly. Make the next ring a bit longer and place it on top of the first, so that the pot becomes wider than the base circumference. Make small serrations with a knife, comb, or fork on top and bottom of the flattened rolls so they will be easier to join. Press the rolls together tightly and smooth out the lines between them with your fingers, inside and outside, as you build up the pot and before the clay becomes too dry.

The coil method was very popular in the past as it allowed a great variety of shapes of bowls and pots. The method is a bit slow, however, since it takes considerable work to smooth out the lines between the rings, especially on the larger pots.

As mentioned earlier, the best way to learn how to work with clay is by starting with small things; less patience is required to make a small object well than a large one and you can get much enjoyment and achieve fascinating results by working with miniature pottery.

It is not difficult to make tiny pitchers and cups, only $\frac{3}{8}$ to $\frac{3}{4}$ inch high, of well-washed potter's clay, which you can buy at many hobby shops or from a ceramic supplier. Make a roll about an inch in diameter, pound it flat with a piece of smooth wood, on a table preferably covered with a piece of paper or plastic so the clay won't

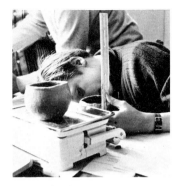

Copies of old clay pots are carefully measured and weighed. The picture is from the pottery workshop at Lejre. For a clay pot you need a lump of clay that weighs one-fifth more than the finished pot.

47

stick to the tabletop. Do not make the clay cake more than $\frac{1}{8}$ inch thick. With a bit of luck, some skill and care, you can easily turn this piece of clay into a small pitcher.

A thin-walled miniature pitcher needs to dry for only about two days, in a room with central heating. Then you can fire it by putting it in an old tin can and, by means of a wire, lowering it onto the coals of a stove. Do not try to fire small clay pots directly in a gas flame or the like. The clay heats too quickly and will burst with small sharp explosions, flinging chips in all directions.

Firing these small items in a real miniature kiln is fun. A small model of the Hasseris kiln (see pages 57–66) made on a scale of 1 to 10, or about 5 inches long, would be perfect. Simply form the kiln of potter's clay with walls about $\frac{5}{16}$ inch thick. Make it in two parts, an upper and a lower, and let them dry for a week. Wattle is not needed. Fill a box, 20 by 20 by 4 inches with sand and press the lower half of the kiln into the sand to half its depth. Place the miniature pots on the elevated firing chamber of the kiln and put on the top. Use charcoal as fuel and light the first coals in an old flower pot, outdoors. Transfer the live coals to the firebox of the miniature kiln with a pair of tweezers and stoke the kiln in the same manner. The charcoal fire must have forced air, and since there is a limit to one's own blowing capacity, we recommend the use of small bellows or a vacuum cleaner. The much more convenient vacuum cleaner may give too much air but the flow can be restricted by a rubber hose of suitable diameter inserted in the exhaust hole of the cleaner.

It takes from half an hour to an hour to bring the kiln to a red-hot glow sufficient for red-firing the small clay pots. The kiln itself will at the same time also be red-fired, so it may be used several times. During the first firing it is advisable to go a little slowly on the stoking to avoid too many cracks in the kiln. Don't put your face too close to the kiln, since sparks can fly out due to the forced air.

Manufacture of earthenware has naturally developed numerous improved methods, such as the potter's wheel and casting. All these methods, however, require special technical equipment that is too expensive for a beginner who just wants to explore the art of the potter and must first get acquainted with clay.

This little model of the Hasseris kiln has been used for firing miniature pots. The model is made in two parts so the top can be laid in place after the kiln is loaded. It is fired with charcoal and heated up by means of a bellows or vacuum cleaner blower.

On the opposite page the most common methods of shaping clay are shown.

Left. The finger method, or Jutland pot method. Only the fingers, and especially the thumb, are used to shape the cylindrical form into a cup or bowl. Even a very large Jutland pot can be made this way.

Right. The coil method. This should be used only for larger pots, especially complicated shapes.

6 Open-pit Firing
Limhamn Kiln

Pottery is the first handicraft—perhaps we should call it the first domestic industry—that developed concurrently with the use of fire. In the kitchen-middens of Denmark there are potsherds more than 5000 years old. They come from the conical-based vessel of the Ertebolle Culture, when people lived as hunters and gatherers and had just begun to keep cattle and domestic animals. The clay pots had thick walls and were built up of layers of clay coils placed one on top of the other. At that time they were mixing the clay with powdered calcined granite.

We can only guess how they fired the clay pots. Of course then, as now, they had traditions and methods that the elders taught the younger.

One can fire clay pots in an open fire, but it must be done very carefully and it takes a long time. First and foremost, the pot must be bone dry—dried in the air for at least one month, until it has a light surface color. Only then can you dry and fire the pot, and this requires several stages. First it must stand near the open fire repeatedly and be preheated on all sides by the radiant heat. Then one can start the firing with a very low fire in a layer of ashes with hot coals. Little by little one can enlarge the fire around the pots. It takes time, and as a rule not even half the pots survive the process intact.

Open-pit firing is far better. It is a firing method that is extremely old, and it has been used in Denmark by the makers of Jutland pots up to the present day. For a skilled stoker, it is not at all difficult, even though there is great risk of burst or stunted pots during the firing. One must realize that the firing temperature as a rule can only get as high as 930 to 1110 °F., so it is only possible to make low-fired pottery by this method. In many cases it is even hard to get the clay pots completely fired.

You must select a high, dry place for the pit, a good distance from buildings and flammable vegetation. Dig a 10-inch-deep hollow about 30 inches in diameter. Then cut about 100 sod blocks and pile them next to the hollow. You will need a bunch of dry straw and about 33 pounds of absolutely dry fuel wood pieces about 2 feet long.

Children firing an open pit. Firing and covering is most exciting, especially since it must all be done in a very few minutes. As soon as the fire has caught, the pit is quickly covered with sod to make it airtight.

Open-pit Firing
Limhamn Kiln

Fill the hollow with straw and lay the bone-dry pots on it, with the openings down. Build the fuel up, around, and over the clay pots like a teepee, about 30 inches high. Finally, place a ring of sod blocks around the whole thing. Now you are ready, but if you have long hair be sure to bind it up with a scarf so you won't get singed.

Light the straw and as soon as the branchwood catches and crackles, cover the whole pyramid with sod blocks within not more than one to two minutes, despite the fire and smoke. Otherwise the pots will burst.

The sod cover must be almost airtight. You must not be able to see the fire but there must be some small cracks in the top, through which the smoke can seep out. It is also necessary to have vent holes at the bottom; as a matter of fact they are almost impossible to avoid, but be careful that there are not too many—two to three small holes are enough.

You must observe the firing constantly for the first four to five hours, because the fuel can collapse as well as the sod. You must repair any cracks or breaks in the covering with new sod.

After five hours, cover all cracks and openings with dirt and sand and leave it alone until the next day.

Opening the pit is the most exciting part of all. However, you must wait until all the fuel has been consumed. Preferably, it should be

A group of Jutland pots placed for open-pit firing. These had first been smoked in a smoke oven and were colored by the process.

done in two or three stages, so the cooling will not occur too quickly. It is best to lift the hot pots up and place them on top of the ashes and let them cool there gradually. Do not place the hot clay pots on moist soil—and never open the pit during rain.

A really good, airtight open-pit firing produces completely black pottery, but normally you end up with red-and-black mottled earthenware, which of course has a charm of its own.

As mentioned, the raw pots must be bone dry. The old Jutland potter women often dried their pots for two to three months, usually on iron rods over the hearth; in many primitive potteries it was customary to scorch the earthenware pots by baking them in an open fire before the actual firing, to make sure they would be completely dry before going into the open pit or a regular kiln. You can follow the same principle nowadays but shorten the procedure and at the same time insure a good result by pre-drying the pottery for about two hours in an ordinary baking oven at 390 °F.

Our ancestors improved the open-pit firing method very quickly. Almost 4500 years ago a clever tribe lived in Skaane and on Zealand. They may have migrated from the east or they may have been native inhabitants who, under favorable living conditions combined with the presence of skilled craftsmen, developed a "culture." This culture

Open-pit Firing
Limhamn Kiln

A fired open pit is uncovered and the pots, which were successful here, are carefully lifted out to cool. All coals must be burned out before uncovering the pit.

This is the oldest form of pottery in Denmark. From the Ertebølle dwelling place on Gudsø Fiord.

was characterized by decorated, hard-fired pottery and finely made, serrated flint weapons. This tribe is referred to as the "Pitted Ware Group" because they often decorated their pottery with small finger impressions.

Sture Silow excavated a "kiln" from this period at Limhamn in Skaane. It is somewhere in between an open pit and an ordinary kiln, but differs from the open pit by having permanent air vents in the bottom through four underground air canals.

The Limhamn pit kiln is constructed as a small stone-lined hollow in the ground, 12 to 16 inches wide with four $2\frac{3}{4}$-inch-diameter air canals made partially of stone. A firing canal leads from under the center of the kiln to the clay pit at the side (see diagram). The kiln stones may be held together with clay. The kiln was probably covered with sod and sand during the firing.

Only a few sods are necessary for each firing. That was certainly important when there were no iron spades for digging sod blocks. Imagine the difficulty of digging up sod with a wooden spade or one made from the shoulder blade of an ox!

The Limhamn kiln has been tested at the Center at Lejre and found very reliable. It fired the pottery somewhat harder than the open pit at a little over 1290 °F. firing temperature.

The best firing schedule is as follows: place a small tuft of dry straw (or crumpled newspaper) where the firing canal leads into the bottom of the kiln and on that place about 3 or 4 pounds of charcoal. Then load the pit kiln with the pottery and place the dry wood fuel in between until the hollow is filled to a little above the ground surface. Cover the whole thing with sod and sand, making it completely airtight except for a thin tube that you may push through the top to see if there is smoke when the fire is lighted. Close this hole as soon as the fire has caught.

Firing through the long, narrow firing canal may cause a problem, but you can solve this most easily by using a thin, twisted wisp of straw or a lighter made of folded paper. (Actually, you can get by with a shorter firing canal than was used in the original kiln.) As soon as you see that the fire has caught, by smoke seeping out of the side vents and the top hole, close the firing canal airtight with stone and clay. The Limhamn kiln burns very slowly and it must burn that way to achieve the best results.

At the Limhamn kiln site several flat lumps of clay were used to cover the vent holes. The experiments at Lejre indicate that two of the vent holes should be covered during the first hour and then the pit kiln could be left unattended until the next day. Just as for the open-pit firing, the Limhamn pit kiln requires about twenty-four hours' firing before it can be opened. Using bone-dry raw pottery, with practice

54

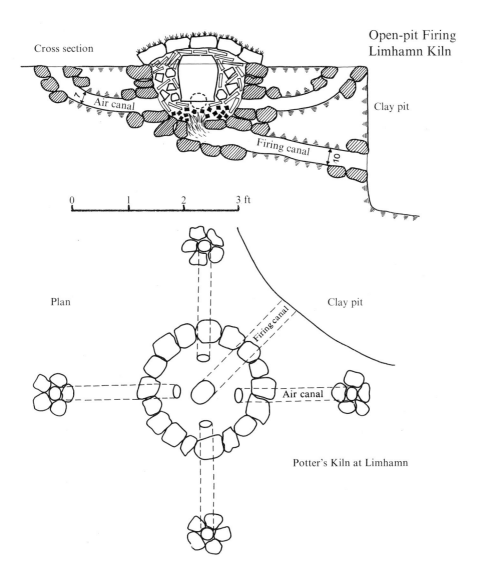

Open-pit Firing
Limhamn Kiln

Cross section

Air canal

Clay pit

Firing canal

10

0   1   2   3 ft

Plan

Clay pit

Firing canal

Air canal

Potter's Kiln at Limhamn

55

The Limhamn kiln here being constructed. The stone-lined pit is cemented with clay. In the picture, two boys are shown digging the four air canals leading to the fire base.

Preparing a firing of the Limhamn kiln. A little charcoal is placed in the kiln bottom and the clay pots and fuel are placed on top. The air canal has to be cleaned out and the whole covered with a layer of sod.

you may be able to obtain up to 90 per cent unbroken hard-fired pottery from this kiln.

One drawback of the open pit and the pit kiln is that fire and coals touch the pottery during firing. Often a clay pot is heated so intensely at one spot by a charcoal ember that it cracks because of too much stress in the material.

This condition has been considerably improved through the "invention" of a kiln like the Hasseris kiln, described in the next chapter. Fire, coals, and pottery are in the same space but are kept separate so that direct contact between the fire and the pots can be avoided. This accounts for the much smaller loss in this kiln than in the pit kiln. The Glostrup kiln provides an even greater assurance of successful firing because the fire and pottery are located in separate spaces. The pottery is then in contact only with the hot flue gases. The construction of this kiln is really also much more industrial. It can be loaded with larger quantities of pottery and is a more permanent type. It may be used more than thirty times without substantial repairs, and when necessary, repairs are easily carried out.

7   Hasseris Kiln

The potter's kiln at the old grave pit near Hasseris was excavated by
Mr. Marseen, assistant curator at the Historical Museum in Aalborg.
The kiln was found collapsed over nine clay pots, the last firing before
the kiln had been abandoned because of some mishap. Mr. Marseen
has reconstructed the kiln and carried out a successful firing in it.

At the Center at Lejre we resumed the experiments with the kiln
with excellent results. The kiln is easy to build, easy to work with, and
it yields fine results provided you do not make any serious mistakes.
In several firings, the entire firing was flawless.

Although the kiln at the Hasseris site contained clay pots from the
Germanic Iron Age, 500 A.D., this type of kiln is considerably older
than that. A find near the city of Schleswig, excavated for the Museum
of Gottorp Castle, indicates that it was known in the Celtic Iron Age,
about 200 B.C. A kiln of exactly the same form as the Hasseris kiln
was excavated at Tuse Naes in Uglerup, Denmark, in the summer of
1967, by the Holbaek Museum. The Uglerup kiln was, however, built
of large brick *munkesten* from the fourteenth century and the use of
the kiln is not certain, but it shows that this kiln design was so excellent
that the type has remained in Denmark for at least about 2000 years.

At the Center in Lejre the Hasseris kiln was constructed in six or
seven hours by five young people. We were lucky enough to have the
necessary materials at hand. We used two or three wheelbarrow-loads
of ordinary sand containing clay (not too lean), 20 $\frac{3}{4}$-inch willow
twigs cut about 50 inches long, 20 $\frac{3}{8}$-inch osiers about 60 inches long,
and 50 sod blocks for insulating the clay dome.

We outlined the oven shape according to the diagram and dug the
figure-eight-shaped hole. At Lejre we have clay soil so we did not
need to shore up the sides of the hole. In sandy soil one must plaster
the walls of the kiln chamber with 2 or 3 inches of daub, and the sides
of the ash pit must be supported with sod blocks.

Along the upper part of the kiln chamber we dug a 4- by 4-inch
ledge as a support for the dome.

When constructing a Hasseris kiln, brace the dome vault with an
interlacing of willow twigs. First mount all the transverse arches of

Hasseris Kiln

Lighting the Hasseris kiln.

The diagrams on the opposite page show the Hasseris kiln. Lower left. The kiln door is built up with turf blocks. It is made airtight with earth or rubble and clay. Side walls are of wattle covered with clay. Lower right. Cross section of kiln. Dome is of clay spread over a wattle mesh. For lathing, use straw or dock leaves. A flue hole 4 by 4 inches is at the back of the kiln.

the twigs and adjust the heights to assure a nice, evenly rounded dome over the fireplace, with a rise of 8 to 12 inches in the middle. Then weave the osiers lengthwise, making a 3- by 4-inch mesh. In this way you will get a good supporting frame for the clay.

Then cover the entire mesh with a tight lathing of straw such as was used at Hasseris, or with dock leaves such as we used.

The clay for the wall is ordinary sand containing moraine clay. Mix it by kneading with water until it has the consistency of thick oatmeal and plaster it on the lathing in a 3- to 4-inch-thick layer. Pack it tightly by beating and smoothing. Pound and squeeze the base portion very thoroughly to make it completely airtight and strong. It is very important that the edge of the kiln is airtight all the way around to avoid treacherous air in the kiln, which can discolor the clay pots. The front of the oven is finished with an opening large enough for the clay pots that will go into the kiln. The opening should not be narrower than 12 inches.

The clay dome must now air dry. It is, of course, best to build in the

58

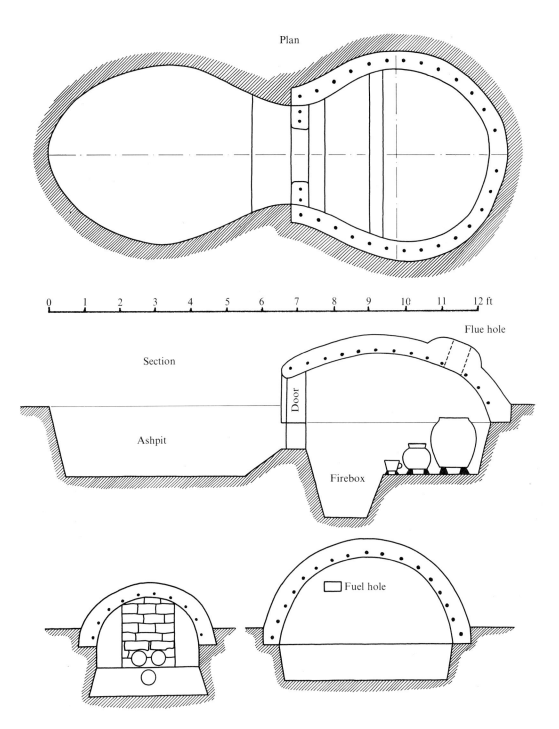

Plan

0   1   2   3   4   5   6   7   8   9   10   11   12 ft

Section

Flue hole

Door

Ashpit

Firebox

Fuel hole

These pictures show the main stages in building a Hasseris kiln. The crew shown here built this kiln in about six hours. First the figure-eight shape was dug. Osiers and clay were gathered and brought to the site. The osiers were braided in a mesh dome shape over the kiln and covered with dock leaves. Then, clay was kneaded with water, in a wheelbarrow, and packed and shaped on the dome. The last picture shows the kiln nearly finished: now it only needs to dry for a week before the first firing to form a tight dome, after that it is ready for use.

spring, and you must protect it from rain with a tarpaulin or a large piece of plastic. It is not advisable to light a low fire in the kiln because it is too easy to burn up the meshwork.

Avoiding cracking in the clay is probably impossible, so cracks will have to be repaired with a thin paste of clay of the same type as described above. It will probably be necessary to repair it at least twice during the drying period.

When the clay is completely dry and so hard that it can withstand pressure, you can fire the kiln. You must use an intense fire. This will take from 18 to 27 cubic feet of dry wood. The dome has to be fired as thoroughly as possible until it is partially or wholly tile. At first, leave the outside uncovered to evaporate the water in the clay and repair possible cracks with a clay slurry. During the last half of the firing cover the dome with insulation of sod or sand. Thus the clay retains the heat better and becomes more thoroughly fired. If one fires pots in the kiln before the kiln is dry, the clay "boils" out and loses its carrying capacity, the mesh burns and the dome collapses.

At the test firing of the Hasseris kiln at the site of the find, the kiln reached 1470 °F. after approximately eighteen hours of stoking and the earthenware was completely fired without cracks.

At Lejre we have experimented some more with firings for two reasons. First, to make different types: red-fired and black-fired or mottled pottery. Second, we succeeded in reducing the firing time, since it is very difficult to get help for the lengthy stoking duty at the kiln. Our success was especially due to the fact that the kiln had already been cured and was ready for use. We always make sure that the kiln is dried out the day before the firing by making a small fire in it. There was no roof over the kiln because we worked only during the summer months and were lucky enough to have dry weather. During rainy periods you need a roof. An excavation of a fragmentary kiln at Jerslev close to Hjørring, Denmark, clearly shows post holes for a roof that had obviously been erected over the kiln.

The most common firing of earthenware today, as in the past, is the red firing. This is very simple to do in the Hasseris kiln. The raw pottery must be absolutely bone dry; the pots will have to dry for approximately one month in a heated room around 68 °F. with ventilation, or you can store them in a drying cupboard or in a drying room. If the thickness of the clay is more than $\frac{3}{8}$ inch the drying period must be extended.

Insert the clay pots in the oven with the opening up or to the side, preferably not with the bottom up. Larger pots are best supported on three sherds to get heat underneath. Place smaller pots inside larger.

The kiln entrance must be partially closed. Have about seventy sod blocks and three to four drain pipes lying ready at the side of the kiln

Inside the Hasseris kiln after hand firing various clay pieces at about 1290 °F.

for this. The firing should be slow, started with shavings or paper, dry kindling, and two or three large pieces of wood. Never use kerosene. It will increase the heat too quickly since the heating value of liquid fuel is about twice that of wood. During the first two hours maintain a slow fire because the pottery must dry out slowly. By cautiously stoking through the open front door of the kiln, the temperature will not reach much above 250 °F., which is enough to evaporate completely the water from the pottery without bursting it.

After two or three hours, gradually stoke the fire a bit faster but still keeping it moderate. The kiln temperature must not go above 660 to 750 °F. during the first four hours. You may determine the temperature with a Tempil pellet or Tempilaq line on a potsherd, which will melt at a given temperature. The pellet or the sherd may be placed inside a spy hole in the kiln or attached to a pole and held in the kiln for a few minutes. We can only speculate on how our ancestors controlled the heat in the kilns or if they just fired the clay pots according to a certain schedule, the details of which were taught from master to apprentice. Of course, an experienced stoker may fairly well estimate the heat in the kiln by slipping a dry stick of a certain kind of wood in through the flue hole and then counting the seconds until the stick catches. Still, we don't know about this. As a matter of fact, an experienced stoker who knows his kiln will ordinarily know about the temperature level of the kiln without being able to say why. It may well have been quite unnecessary for the old fire attendants or stokers to have any kind of thermometer for checking the fire. The stokers at the firing of the old Jutland pots never heard of a thermometer; they just fired the pots according to an inherited system that is now partially forgotten.

62

Hasseris Kiln

The Hasseris kiln is ready for use. The opening is half-closed with turf and the drain pipes for air are in place.

When you start the more intense stoking, close up the stoke hole three-quarters of the way with sod. Position the drain pipes to make a draft in the kiln at the bottom of the stoke hole, meticulously fill the interspace between the drain pipes tightly with clay or soil and make a clay plug for each pipe. This way you can regulate the draft and insure that the temperature does not increase too quickly. At this state of the firing the kiln must have draft from one or two drain pipes. You must also make sure that the fire does not burn out—the pottery must not be exposed to great temperature drops or it will become stratified, which might cause cleavage in the body and ultimate splitting of the pots. You must stoke gradually during this entire period by adding wood pieces one at a time at suitable intervals.

This entire pre-firing period lasts about four hours. Then you can begin to force the stoking. Fill up the firebox with fuel. There must be a draft from at least three drain pipes, and you must close the stoke hole completely between stokings, now done with many pieces of wood instead of one at a time.

In Lejre, we have measured the temperatures with modern thermo-electric pyrometers, which of course did not exist in the past. The Romans, in a pottery near Pula on Sardinia, did have a type of clay pretzel that they fished out of a hole in the kiln with a pole so they could determine the temperature. This technique might have been

63

Black pottery fired in the Hasseris kiln.

Present-day copies of black clay pots from the Iron Age made at the Center at Lejre. Fired in Hasseris kiln.

People who lived in the country did not want to be behind city dwellers, with their fashionable cast-brass candlesticks. Brass was expensive, so the Jutland potter women made clay copies.

known in Denmark, but no evidence has been found in the excavations. Moreover, measuring temperature isn't that important with a Hasseris kiln. You can see the pots through the draft hole, and from this you can determine the temperature, as experienced kiln attendants do, by looking at the glowing pot colours;

Weak red-black glows at about 1020 °F.

Cherry-red color corresponds to a bit over 1200 °F.

Red-orange is reached at 1380 °F.

The white-hot glow is first reached at 1830 °F.

We cannot reach a temperature of 1830 °F. in this kiln, using wood. It is possible to "fish" a clay cup out through the stoke hole with a wooden stick to see if it's "had enough." You must not let the cup cool off too much, or it can't be replaced in the kiln without damage.

Based on experience, it takes in all seven or eight hours to reach up to 1290–1470 °F. with this firing schedule. When you have reached this temperature, hold it for half an hour and close the stoke hole completely. Open the draft hole and allow the oven to burn out. Do not cool the pottery too fast. Remember that the pots cannot tolerate moisture or rain as you remove them.

Mottled firing: if you want to have pottery with a mottled black-and-red surface, you must close the vent holes (drain pipes) after the first half of the firing to accomplish a partial reducing in the last phase of the firing. Reducing is incomplete combustion of the fuel caused by too little air to charcoal ratio so that the atmosphere of the oven becomes saturated with carbon monoxide (CO) instead of with carbon dioxide (CO_2) plus a possible excess of oxygen. Also, if you push part of the charcoal from the firebox in between the pots during the last stoking, the carbon monoxide formation occurs very close to the

64

Figure-eight-shaped kiln built of large used bricks with clay mortar, 12th to 13th century. Found at Uglerup at Tuse Naes, Denmark. The kiln was dome-shaped with a little deeper and larger stone-lined firebox.

surface of the pots. Some of them will then become completely black. If you want the pottery to be completely black with a red body, at the last stoking, just before the closing of the kiln, stoke with strongly smoking bark or heath peat, possibly drenched with whale oil, tallow, or waste oil, which will soot a lot when it doesn't get much air for combustion. After such a stoking you must completely close all the vent holes and the flue hole to prevent the charcoal in the firebox from flaming up again, which would make the layer of soot on the clay pots turn red once more.

Black firing: the very large pottery with a gray body, and even the Jutland pots, are easily fired in the Hasseris kiln; in ancient times this firing was probably the most often used in this kiln.

The pottery must be well dried and you may even smoke it by warming and pre-drying it in a smoking chamber or above a hearth so that it blackens, as some of the old Jutland potters did. But it is not necessary.

A black firing must remain smoking and reducing throughout. Therefore, when the kiln has been loaded with the pottery, fill up the

65

Hasseris Kiln   firebox completely with dry wood and from 5 to 10 pounds of charcoal. Close the stoke hole with clay or tile fragments and clay mortar and daub the edges tightly. Insert two drain pipes at the very bottom of the stoke hole. When the fuel has been built up correctly, with room for kindling and straw at the back of one of the air holes, you can successfully fire the kiln by inserting an ordinary twist of paper or straw through the drain pipe. Within a quarter of an hour the fire will have caught well and the air will now have to be restricted as much as possible. At the most, only one-half of one of the air pipes may remain open, and the kiln must continuously smoke well out through the flue hole. If the smoke stops, stoke with more green wood. Beech branches with bark are excellent fuel. The temperature must not exceed 570 °F. after four or five hours.

After this pre-firing, the entire bottom of the firebox should be filled with a thick layer of glowing charcoal. Again fill up the firebox with green wood, close the stoke hole airtight, but open up both the air pipes to increase the fire and hence the temperature. The kiln must smoke at all times, and it is possible that you will either have to decrease the air or stoke a couple of extra times. Clear, vibrating air above the flue hole means that the pottery may begin to red fire, and since that was not the intention you must stoke again and damp the air. After a total of seven to ten hours' firing the pottery will start to glow with a dark cherry-red hue—then you must close the flue hole airtight with a rock and clay or soil, while leaving one of the air holes (drain pipes) halfway or completely open for another thirty to sixty minutes. The temperature in the kiln should have reached 1200 °F. Then everything must be closed and the entire front end of the kiln covered airtight with sand and soil. The fire has been smothered, but this type of kiln always has some stray drafts that keep fanning the embers. When you dig out the fire door the next day there is great danger that the charcoal layer will begin to glow again. In such case you must immediately cover the charcoal with sand before you start to empty the kiln. By this time the pottery should be completely hard-fired and black. It must be cooled slowly and will not tolerate water for two or three hours after the unloading.

The Hasseris kiln is easy to work with. You can follow the standard firing process, and there are also many possibilities for variation which you may not always be able to manage in the beginning, but after you have familiarized yourself with the kiln, it is easy to gain experience and fun to experiment. You can get good results without any additional expense, other than fuel. This kiln has served our ancestors for hundreds of years, and thanks to the archaeologists it has been brought to our attention again. It is a pity that it was forgotten so long.

66

8   Glostrup Kiln

When you look at the collections of pottery from the past in Danish and other museums, you will readily note that our most skillful potters lived about 2000 years ago, at the end of the Celtic and beginning of the Roman Iron Age. Without technical aids such as the potter's wheel, they produced small, fine cups, thin and smooth as porcelain, and handsome well-formed earthenware pots in all sizes and shapes; these were often made without decoration, but they had well-treated varied surfaces of many types. They made pottery objects for all purposes: fine service of thin, black-red ceramics; beautiful, distinctively shaped goblets and bowls—presumably for table setting; large, beautifully formed pitchers with highly varied surface treatment from velvet-smooth black to coarse Pompeian-red surface; stoneware and fired yellow ware. They made coarse kitchen utensils and large brewing vats, $31\frac{1}{2}$ by $23\frac{5}{8}$ inches, with thick walls, and enormous grain-storage vessels about 5 feet high. The potters could make every kind of domestic utensil. They were professionals who engaged mainly in pottery and had their own workshops with their own kiln plant and clay pits. We found this kind of plant when a building was being constructed on Banemarksvej in Glostrup. Here lay a 2000-year-old town under the residential area that stretches from Hederavej to the new freight yard. We were lucky and found most of the pottery and were permitted to help dig it out. There were traces of several deep, natural clay pits with fine blue clay, and we found many dug pits with prepared potter's clay, wedged and containing wood ash, ready for use today. Even underneath the floor in the potter's workshop there were pits with potter's clay ready for use. Blue clay mixed with wood ash was used for the finer objects. This mixture was aggregated with powdered calcined granite for larger items—in certain cases mica, sorted out of the calcined granite, was added to the finer earthenware. We found some caches of clean-picked mica, apparently stored in bags that had rotted away a long time ago. The village appears to have been burned down and laid waste about 200 or 300 A.D.

The kiln plants lay approximately 100 to 130 feet from the houses.

It is not difficult to build a Glostrup
kiln, even though it does not use brick
and mortar. A skeleton is woven of
willow branches, then clay is daubed
on both sides of this mesh. The clay
cracks during drying, but can be
repaired with clay slurry. Finally the
kiln is fired with a strong firing. It is a
simple construction method that had
been used for a long time, but unfortunately had been forgotten until
now.

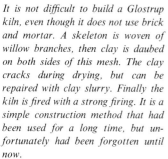

There was a deep-lying, stone-built fireplace with long heat canals leading out to the sides; we never found out what they had been used for. Then there was a 2-foot-thick layer of kiln remains, built one on top of the other. This was also impossible to interpret. A little distance away, however, was the bottom of a kiln with two fireplaces. There was no mystery about this kiln, and it is the one that has been reconstructed at the Center at Lejre.

The kiln from Glostrup is rather complicated, but very effective and spacious. The builders were professional potters who built it for a specific purpose, and its crooked form indicates that it had been under a roof. We found no trace of this, however. A similar type excavated at Jerslev in the county of Hjørring, Denmark, showed several post holes around it, so that one did have a roof over it, which is essential if you want to work with the kiln during the winter or on rainy days. This kiln also was built with clay and wide-mesh wattle—the best construction material available for kilns at that time. During the reconstruction at Lejre, we discovered how to build a kiln almost identical to the Glostrup kiln. We have carried out numerous firings of pottery in it, normally with good results.

To build this type of kiln, you must dig the two deep fireplaces first. Remove all the sod from the kiln area and pile it up where the chimney will be.

Make the wattle preferably of $\frac{3}{8}$ inch- by $1\frac{1}{4}$-inch-thick willow branches. The vertical supports should be the thickest and bound together at the top ridge with a string around a supporting branch laid horizontally. This makes the construction rigid and sturdy. Then weave the horizontal osiers in between the vertical branches to give the network a mesh of 4 by 4 inches.

Use ordinary sand containing or mixed with moraine clay kneaded by foot with water to a rather stiff, porridge consistency. Be sure that while daubing you pound it good and tight around the wattle with your closed fists from both sides. In this kiln the wattle must lie in the middle of the clay. Collect about two half-wheelbarrow loads of 4-inch rocks from the fields; do not use flint because it bursts during heating. The rocks are for a grate on the bottom of the fireplace and as a lining in the fire channel leading into the kiln chamber. There must be about two to three hundred sod blocks for the chimney and insulation.

Sod is excellent for building the chimney and holds up astonishingly well, even though it does not comply with modern fire regulations. Our ancestors' chimney construction, therefore, may only be built far from modern houses. Of course the sod will crumble with repeated use, but if you line the chimney by plastering on a layer of clay, it will last for at least thirty or forty firings.

Glostrup Kiln   You can build the kiln in about one hundred working hours, including digging the clay and sod, if they exist at the site.

After the daubing with clay, the kiln must air dry for a week or two, and during that time you will have to repair the cracks in the clay with a half-dry slurry. The drying may be advanced if you light a slow fire in the kiln a few times.

When the clay is dry, the kiln is fired with intense stoking in both fireplaces for three or four hours. In the beginning this is done without insulation, because you will still have to repair the cracks, but after an hour or two, you should cover the entire kiln with sod. The kiln door must be clay-daubed during the firing.

Since the kiln has a peculiarly asymmetrical design, larger firings must await a favourable wind, one from the southwest if the kiln lies north–south with the chimney facing north. If so, you can actually force the kiln all the way up to 1830 °F. in five hours.

The firing schedule for the Glostrup kiln is difficult to explain. At Lejre we have fired it approximately fifty times, using the two kilns, and have determined that you can get them to burn with anything if you just have a bit of experience. If, however, we must guess about our ancestors' firing schedule, this is how we believe the kiln should be used:

After stacking the kiln, seal the hatch with clay fragments and clay mortar and insulate with sod.

The side fireplace is stoked for three or four hours, initially low but later intensely. In the meantime, the main fireplace is packed tightly with dry, thick wood.

After a good three hours the fuel that lies closest to the kiln chamber in the main fireplace is just about ready to burst into flames. At this point light the main fireplace in the side that is closest to the direction of the wind and close the side fireplace tightly with sod and dirt. The main fireplace will blaze intensely for about three hours and the temperature in the kiln will reach about 1200 to 1290 °F. Many Iron Age pots were fired at that temperature.

You can easily increase the firing temperature and get hard-fired earthenware by stoking the main fireplace two or three times—1470 to 1830 °F. is easily reached.

If the main fireplace is completely or halfway open, you get red or yellow pottery like ordinary oxidized ware. The oxidizing firing occurs with an ample supply of oxygen; reducing firing occurs with a limited supply of oxygen.

To obtain black or mottled earthenware you must close the chimney tightly with a fireproof plate when the pottery starts to glow. You can use a sheet of iron, a discarded earthenware pot, or a wash basin. Then you must close the openings of both main fireplaces with

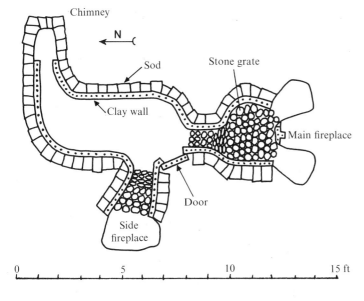

Glostrup Kiln

Potter's kiln from Glostrup. Roman
Iron Age, around 200 A.D.

71

Glostrup Kiln

sod and dirt. For black firing, you must further make sure that the cracks in the kiln are sealed and that any existing spy holes are closed airtight. The black vitrification of the clay starts at about 1110 °F., so you mustn't wait too long to start the reducing firing.

It is also possible to fire glazed pottery in the Glostrup kiln, and with great success. The loss is small. You must realize that the flue gases pass directly through the kiln, so the glazed ware becomes similar to that of the Middle Ages, quite varied, mottled, and flecked, which has a unique appeal. First or biscuit firing of the pottery is done as an ordinary oxidizing red firing.

In firing glazed objects the kiln must be absolutely dry. Therefore,

Glostrup kiln. Half has been daubed with clay and has stood for several days drying. The cracks in the clay are being repaired. Notice that the cracks are nearly parallel and about 10 inches apart.

the day before we generally made a low fire in the kiln. For a glaze firing that must reach as high as 1830 °F. the wind must be absolutely favorable. In this case the firing starts with the usual slow stoking in the side fireplace, increasing over three hours. Then the main fireplace is started. Keep stoking slowly in the side fireplace for five hours after you have lit the fire. From then on you can push the fire in both fireplaces, and by using high-quality fuel you might bring the temperature to 1830 °F. within seven or eight hours after starting.

In removing glazed pieces, especially, you must cool the pots gradually and be careful not to remove them in rain or dampness.

As we have cautioned a number of times before, never use kerosene

Glostrup Kiln

Glostrup kiln drying. Cracks have been repaired and the kiln covered with an insulating layer of turf.

A Glostrup kiln is easy to repair. After several firings, a piece of this wall developed too many cracks. Here it is being fixed.

In sandy parts of Denmark where clay was lacking, kilns were built of stone with clay domes. This one from Ovdrup in Jutland was found about 165 feet from some house ruins.

(paraffin) in the old potters' kilns. One of the few times we had broken pottery in the Glostrup kiln was the day we used kerosene for lighting. The heat gets too intense at the beginning.

The first firing in the Glostrup kiln requires about $\frac{2}{3}$ to 1 cubic yard of wood, and since the construction costs for the kiln are so low, the cost of work in the kiln can be kept at a reasonable level. Of course it is not as cheap as working with the Hasseris kiln or the earth kiln.

Kilns were not always built of clay. In a very sandy region at Ovtrup, between Nibe and Løgstør, Denmark, a nice little dome-shaped kiln was found built of granite stones from the area. The fireplace may have been covered with a clay dome. Material available at the site was used and the potters became accustomed to what was there; transportation possibilities were limited in those days. Further-more, it's very possible that a "travelling apprentice" may have reached the far south, where he saw the stone-built Roman kilns. Our technical methods, quite naturally, were strongly influenced by those of neighbouring countries, perhaps to a much greater degree than we imagine today.

9 St. Olai Kiln

Perhaps we should not write about this kiln yet, because our experiments at Lejre have not been completely successful. On the other hand, we have got far enough with a few halfway good experiments to know how the kiln was used, and we therefore feel justified in describing it here.

During an excavation undertaken for the Historical Museum of Vendsyssel, Denmark, we found a buried brick kiln in the midst of a site from the Iron Age in St. Olai parish near Hjørring. The kiln was from the time when brickmakers were itinerant craftsmen travelling from place to place to fire bricks for peasants and large landowners. They were in demand in all parts of the country, because it was becoming fashionable to modernize housing by building brick chimneys for stoves and ranges instead of open fireplaces with louvers.

Judging from the type of brick, this excavated kiln is not very old; presumably it is from the eighteenth century, although the working method was probably known from the time people first began to use brick in Denmark, 900 years ago.

The brick kiln was simply a rectanglar 4-foot-deep hole in the ground with a long stoking canal. The subsoil at the locality consisted of well-draining sandy soil. At Lejre we duplicated the kiln in clay soil, which contains much more moisture than sandy soil. The test firings, therefore, weren't entirely successful at first.

The old brickmakers used to find a place with fine brick clay and then work there. They dug the clay, wedged it, molded bricks in wooden forms, and laid them to dry in the sun. Then they dug the rectangular hole for the kiln and the 9- to 13-foot-long stoking canal. The kiln chamber had a level brick floor with a sunken air canal in the center.

The three solid walls were lined with broken brick to the thickness of a quarter-brick. The front wall of the kiln was laid as a half-brick wall with a well-built stoke opening.

If you want to make the kiln yourself, the entire front wall can be laid from unfired brick—made *in situ*—with a thick clay slurry as

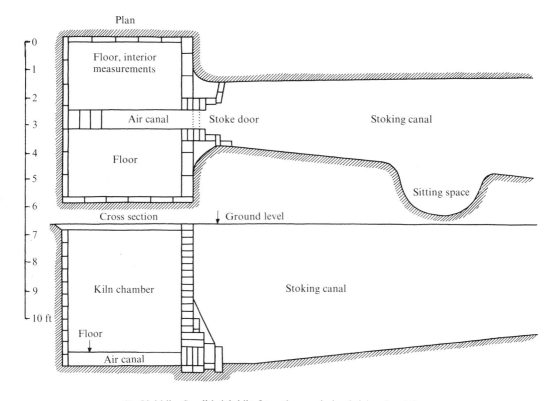

Plan

Floor, interior measurements

Air canal   Stoke door   Stoking canal

Floor

Stoking canal

Sitting space

Cross section   ↓ Ground level

Kiln chamber   Stoking canal

Floor

Air canal

0
1
2
3
4
5
6
7
8
9
10 ft

St. Olai kiln. Small brick kiln from the wandering brickmakers' time

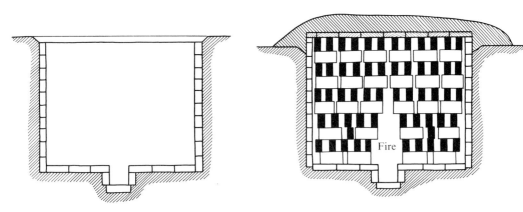

Cross section of empty kiln   Cross section of filled kiln with unfired brick

Fire

St. Olai Kiln

St. Olai kiln seen from inside, empty. Exterior walls here are made of discarded bricks with clay mortar. The air canal leads from the stoke hole.

St. Olai brick kiln in use. The kiln is filled and covered with unfired bricks. Firing has just started, but the kiln has not yet been covered with earth.

St. Olai Kiln   mortar. This was almost always used for the old kilns. It is an excellent
method of making kiln walls and was used right up to our grand-
parents' time. Both brick and clay mortar vitrify well together at the
first firing and crack only slightly. Cracks can easily be repaired with
clay mortar.

The kiln must be completely dry before use. This is best done by
making an ordinary fire on the kiln floor before the unfired bricks are
put in. The bricks, after having been air dried sufficiently for firing,
are stacked in the kiln. Stacking is by far the most important step,
because the quality of the firing depends on the stacking system. First
and foremost, make the fire chamber by stacking the unfired brick in
the kiln over the air canal to form a pyramidal firing chamber about
14 inches wide and 24 inches high. The sides of the fire chamber must
be open everywhere so the heat can move out from the center and
reach between all the bricks.

Stack the bricks so that the space between them is as large as a
brick. Place the bricks on their sides in long parallel rows, each layer
in the kiln perpendicular to the layer underneath so the fire and heat
can reach each stone on all sides. (Remember, bricks have six sides.)
Cover the top layer of unfired brick with a layer of brick set solid,
lying on their flat side. This is covered with a layer of clay or soil 2 to
4 inches thick. At each of the corners of the kiln, make a flue hole
approximately 5 by 10 inches and place a couple of loose bricks next
to them so you can regulate the draft completely or partially by
covering the holes.

The firing is done with wood and you must stoke so intensely that
there is a flaming fire all the time. When there is too much charcoal in
the bottom of the air canal, rake the hot coals out into the side holes
of the firing canal or pull part of them out through the stoke door.
Level the bed of coals and stoke with more wood.

There should not be too fast a draft in through the stoke door
because the incoming air cools the kiln. Try to restrict the air that is
sucked in to just the right amount required to keep a flaming fire
going. Keep the size of the flue holes to a minimum.

Stoking time for the kiln is from sixteen to twenty-four hours and
the bricks must be completely white-hot, approximately 2000 °F.,
before you are finished.

The kiln can fire 700 or 800 ordinary size bricks or 600 large bricks
(*munkesten*). Most of them will be fired quite nicely, especially the
munkesten. One firing takes from $4\frac{1}{2}$ to 9 cord feet of wood, so it is
not quite as economical as the modern brick kilns of today or as the
large kilns from the monastic period. But if you want a small quantity
of special bricks of an old type for some repair, or if you want to make
your own bricks for a grill or fireplace, the St. Olai kiln is excellent.

St. Olai Kiln

Many handicrafts other than pottery were also done in these bygone days. Here is a little bronze sculpture showing a group of smiths at work with a primitive forge and bellows.

Fire and Fire Prevention

We have discussed primitive food preparation and heating with open fireplaces in houses and huts, and with our present-day knowledge we understand the extreme risks of fire in the open-hearth Iron Age house. After bitter experience our ancestors also understood. They built brick chimneys over the fireplaces. They modernized farms by building stove-chambers with stoking canals to jamb stoves or bake ovens. Many housing improvements were made after the discovery of brick. But not everyone was willing to work or spend money to prevent fires, and so society assumed responsibility and officials had to establish laws to regulate the use of fire.

Such laws are necessary in a society. King Valdemar II's Jutland Law, the first Danish law written in the old legal style using legal customs, decisions, and decrees, in Vordingborg 1241, contains the following on fire:

"If the Heath Burns—

"If one sets fire to the heath and burns some man's garden, either heather or peat, or if the fire spreads into the forest and burns and lays waste, the person who set the fire is responsible for the damage even if he had not intended to burn anything except his own property. If the fire spreads to the village, the same applies. If a shepherd or another hired hand, not in the farmer's domain, causes the fire which does the damage, the farmer is not responsible for paying for that . . .

"It is better that no man sets fire in the heath if all the owners are not there together and agree to burn either the bog or heath. Then they themselves can go along and watch the fire so that it does not come into another man's field and cause him damage."

This law was valid in Denmark for several hundred years. The law was not changed without specific reasons. As technology and other social developments have made it necessary, the laws have been amended and detailed, step by step, and have unfortunately become more complicated. There now are ordinances about fire in many different laws, but the main ones are in the Fire Services Act and the new building code of June 10, 1960, copies of which are available in any Danish bookstore. As is true of all modern laws, these are detailed and difficult to read fast, but the building code provision for indoor open fireplaces is important to our discussion. In modern homes these must have a flue to the chimney and they must be constructed on an insulated and fireproof base. The most important section of the law states: "All fireplaces and heating plants using smoke ventilation arrangements and chimneys must be built, maintained, and serviced in such a way that fire hazard and danger of poisoning and other nuisances are avoided."

We have a reason for ending with these words from the law, just as we had a reason throughout the book for urging caution with fire and for saying that children should not work with fire without the supervision or participation of adults. Fire is and always will be dangerous, and it is precisely because of this that it is necessary to learn to use it and know its characteristics most thoroughly.

Bibliography

Beard, D. C. *The Book of Camp-Lore and Woodcraft*. New York: Garden City Publishing Co., Inc., 1920.

Becker, C. J. *Mosefundne Lerkar Fra Yngre Stenalder* (with English summary). Copenhagen: Gyldendal, 1948.

Brooklyn Institute of Arts and Sciences: *The Art and Technique of Ceramics*. New York: Brooklyn Museum, 1937.

Considine, R. B. *Man Against Fire*. New York: Doubleday and Co., Inc., 1955.

Hodges, H. W. M. *Artifacts, An Introduction to Primitive Technology*. New York: Praeger, 1969.

Honey, W. B. *The Art of the Potter*. London: Faber & Faber, 1946.

Klindt-Jensen, O. *Denmark Before the Vikings*. New York: Praeger, 1957.

Leach, B. *A Potter's Book*. Florida: Transatlantic Arts Inc., 1962.

Mason, B. S. *The Junior Book of Camping and Woodcraft*. New York: A. S. Barnes & Co., 1943.

Rhodes, D. *Kilns. Design, Construction, and Operation*. New York: Chilton Book Co., 1968.

Rosenthal, E. *Pottery and Ceramics*. London: Penguin Books, 1954.

Shepard, A. O. *Ceramics for the Archaeologist*. Washington: Carnegie Institution of Washington, 1956.

Sparkes, J. C. L. and Gandy, W. *Potters, Their Arts and Crafts*. New York: T. Whittaker, 1897.

Townsend, A. H. *Camping & Scouting Lore*. New York: Harper & Brothers, 1930.

Index

A clay tile from Corinth shows this representation of a potter's kiln.